WOULD YOU RATHER

THE ULTIMATE BOOK OF STUPIDLY SILLY,
THOUGHT PROVOKING AND ABSOLUTELY
HILARIOUS QUESTIONS FOR KIDS, TEENS AND
ADULTS (GAME BOOK GIFT IDEAS)

AMAZING ACTIVITY PRESS

WOULD YOU RATHER...

MOVE TO ANOTHER COUNTRY

- OR -

LIVE WHERE YOU ARE FOREVER?

GO TO SCHOOL IN THE CAR WITH YOUR MOM
AND DAD
- OR -
GO TO SCHOOL WITH YOUR FRIEND ON THE
PUBLIC BUS?

WOULD YOU RATHER...

BLOW A BALLOON TILL IT POPS

- *OR* -

POP A BALLOON WITH SOMETHING SHARP?

BE IN A DANCE CLASS
- *OR* -
BE IN THE CHOIR?

WOULD YOU RATHER...

HAVE NOISY FRIENDS

- *OR* -

HAVE NOSEY FRIENDS?

HAVE ONLY MULTICOLORED CLOTHES
- *OR* -
HAVE ONLY WHITE CLOTHES?

WOULD YOU RATHER...

LIVE WITH GRANDMA

- *OR* -

LIVE WITH YOUR COUSINS?

DRINK CHOCOLATE MILK

- *OR* -

DRINK HOT CHOCOLATE?

WOULD YOU RATHER...

GET ASSIGNMENTS EVERY SINGLE DAY FOR A YEAR

- OR -

BE STUCK IN SCHOOL FOR A YEAR?

HAVE NO NOSE AT ALL

- OR -

HAVE A NOSE AS LONG AS PINOCCHIO'S?

WOULD YOU RATHER...

STAIN YOUR MOUTH WITH CHICKEN SAUCE AND NOT KNOW

- OR -

STAIN YOUR HANDS WITH CHICKEN SAUCE AND NOT HAVE ANYTHING TO CLEAN IT WITH?

LOSE ALL YOUR BABY PICTURES
- OR -
LOSE ALL THE PICTURES FROM YOUR LAST BIRTHDAY?

WOULD YOU RATHER...

HAVE A BABY PEE ON YOU

- *OR* -

HAVE A BABY THROW UP ON YOU?

HAVE REALLY LONG TOENAILS

- *OR* -

HAVE REALLY LONG FINGERNAILS?

WOULD YOU RATHER...

HAVE A CHICKEN LAY EGGS IN YOUR HAIR

- OR -

HAVE A BIRD MAKE A NEST IN YOUR HAIR?

TRAVEL BY AIRPLANE

- OR -

TRAVEL BY HOT AIR BALLOON?

WOULD YOU RATHER...

LIVE ON A HOUSEBOAT

- OR -

LIVE IN A TREE HOUSE?

BE PRANKED

- OR -

BE A WELL-KNOWN PRANKSTER?

WOULD YOU RATHER...

HAVE TO POOP EVERY HOUR

- OR -

HAVE TO PEE EVERY HOUR?

HAVE YOUR OWN A JETPACK

- OR -

HAVE YOUR OWN ROBOT?

WOULD YOU RATHER...

RIDE THE BENCH ON A SPORTS TEAM THAT ALWAYS WINS

- OR -

BE THE STAR PLAYER ON A LOSING SPORTS TEAM AT SCHOOL?

GIVE YOUR ALREADY CHEWED GUM TO SOMEONE ELSE

- OR -

EAT A PIECE OF GUM FROM THE STREET?

WOULD YOU RATHER...

BE STUCK WITH A CLOWN THAT'S QUITE ANNOYING

- *OR* -

BE STUCK IN A ROOM WITH A CLOWN THAT'S NOT FUNNY?

A MAGIC WIZARD

- *OR* -

BE A SUPERHERO?

WOULD YOU RATHER...

HAVE THE POWER TO TRANSFORM INTO A BUTTERFLY

- OR -

TO TRANSFORM INTO AN EAGLE?

GET COTTON CANDY

- OR -

ICE-CREAM AT A PARK?

WOULD YOU RATHER...

MEET A CLOWN

- *OR* -

BE A CLOWN?

HAVE BADLY TRIMMED HAIR
- *OR* -
HAVE SMELLY HAIR?

WOULD YOU RATHER...

EAT FISH THAT'S HALF BURNT

- *OR* -

EAT FISH THAT'S HALF DONE?

HAVE CLAWS AS HANDS

- *OR* -

HOOKS AS A HAND?

WOULD YOU RATHER...

HAVE THE BUTTON ON YOUR JEANS FALL OFF

- *OR* -

HAVE THE ZIP OF YOUR JEANS CUT?

TAKE A DAY TRIP TO THE BEACH

- *OR* -

TAKE A DAY TRIP TO THE ZOO?

WOULD YOU RATHER...

BE THE 1ST FASTEST SWIMMER IN THE WORLD

- OR -

THE 2ND FASTEST RUNNER IN THE WORLD?

BE SUPERMAN'S SIDEKICK

- OR -

BE SPIDERMAN'S SIDEKICK?

WOULD YOU RATHER...

HAVE A HUNDRED MILLION DOLLARS WORTH OF CANDY

- *OR* -

HAVE A MILLION DOLLARS IN PENNIES?

HAVE MILK RUN DOWN YOUR NOSE EVERY TIME YOU LAUGH
- *OR* -
HAVE MILK RUN OUT OF YOUR EYES EVERY TIME YOU CRIED?

WOULD YOU RATHER...

YOUR HANDS GOT DIRTY ALL THE TIME

- OR -

YOUR FEET GOT DIRTY ALL THE TIME?

RIDE ON A LION

- OR -

RIDE ON THE BACK OF A TIGER?

WOULD YOU RATHER...

WAKE UP WITH WINGS

- *OR* -

WAKE UP WITH A TAIL?

WEAR TRENDY SNEAKERS

- *OR* -

WEAR CUTE SHOES?

WOULD YOU RATHER...

BE A PART OF A CIRCUS SHOW

- *OR* -

GO WATCH A CIRCUS SHOW?

LIVE IN A CAVE ALONE

- *OR* -

LIVE IN A CAVE WITH A FRIENDLY BEAR?

WOULD YOU RATHER...

HAVE A HOLE IN YOUR OUTFIT AND NOT NOTICE

- OR -

HAVE A STAIN ON YOUR OUTFIT AND NOT NOTICE?

MAKE BURPS THAT SMELL REALLY BAD
- OR -
MAKE LOUD BURPS THAT ARE HARD TO IGNORE?

WOULD YOU RATHER...

GO OUTSIDE AND PLAY WITH YOUR FRIENDS

- OR -

HAVE YOUR FRIENDS COME OVER?

MEET A FAIRY

- OR -

A GODDESS?

WOULD YOU RATHER...

WEAR DORA THE EXPLORER PAJAMAS

- *OR* -

WEAR SPONGEBOB PAJAMAS?

SHARE YOUR BED WITH SOMEONE WHO FARTS
A LOT
- *OR* -
SHARE YOUR BED WITH SOMEONE WHO PEES
ON THE BED?

WOULD YOU RATHER...

PLAY GAMES ON A PHONE

- OR -

PLAY A BOARD GAME?

BE THE HEAD OF THE FBI FOR THE PRESIDENT

- OR -

BE A SUPERHERO THAT NEVER GAINS

RECOGNITION?

WOULD YOU RATHER...

BE AN INTERNET SENSATION FROM DOING SOMETHING NERDY

- OR -

BE AN INTERNET SENSATION FROM DOING SOMETHING EMBARRASSING?

BRUSH YOUR TEETH USING A BAR OF SOAP

- OR -

BRUSH YOUR TEETH USING TWO-MONTH-OLD MILK?

WOULD YOU RATHER...

NOT HAVE TOILET PAPER WHILE YOU'RE ON THE TOILET SEAT

- OR -

NOT HAVE WATER TO WASH YOUR HANDS WITH AFTERWARD?

BE EATEN BY YOUR DOG

- OR -

HAVE YOUR DIARY READ OUT IN PUBLIC?

WOULD YOU RATHER...

FOLD ALL THE CLOTHES

- OR -

WASH ALL THE DIRTY CLOTHES?

HAVE A SMALL ZIT THAT WON'T GO AWAY

- OR -

HAVE A MASSIVE ZIT THAT WILL POP?

WOULD YOU RATHER...

SLEEP BESIDE A SKUNK

- *OR* -

SLEEP BESIDE A PIG?

BE IN THE DEBATE CLUB
- *OR* -
WATCH A DEBATE?

WOULD YOU RATHER...

BE IN YOUR FAVORITE VIDEO GAME

- *OR* -

BE IN YOUR FAVORITE CARTOON?

GO TO A DANCE WITH SOMEONE WHO HAS
BODY ODOR
- *OR* -
GO TO A DANCE WITH SOMEONE WHO HAS
BAD BREATH?

WOULD YOU RATHER...

MEET A DONKEY THAT TALKS

- *OR* -

MEET A DONKEY THAT WALKS ON TWO LEGS?

BE A BRAIN SURGEON
- *OR* -
BE A SCIENTIST?

WOULD YOU RATHER...

HAVE THE ABILITY TO TALK TO ANIMALS

- *OR* -

BE ABLE TO HEAR ANIMALS TALK?

NEVER GET TO EAT DONUTS FOR THE REST OF
YOUR LIFE
- *OR* -
EAT ONLY DONUTS FOR AN ENTIRE WEEK?

WOULD YOU RATHER...

BE MUCH SHORTER

- OR -

BE MUCH TALLER?

DROP YOUR NEW PHONE DOWN TO THE
TOILET
- OR -
DROP YOUR CHARM BRACELET DOWN THE
SINK?

WOULD YOU RATHER...

HAVE YOUR LEG STUCK IN THE TOILET BOWL

- OR -

HAVE YOUR HANDS STUCK IN THE TOILET BOWL?

SEE A FUNNY VIDEO OF YOUR PARENTS ONLINE

- OR -

SEE A FUNNY VIDEO OF A CLOSE FRIEND ONLINE?

WOULD YOU RATHER...

BE VERY UNPOPULAR

- *OR* -

BE SUPER POPULAR AND BE STALKED BY PAPARAZZI ALL THE TIME?

LOSE YOUR FAVORITE TOY

- *OR* -

LOSE ALL YOUR SAVINGS?

WOULD YOU RATHER...

EAT 1 SPIDER

- *OR* -

A WHOLE BOWL OF WORMS?

WATCH TV IN BED ALONE
- *OR* -
WATCH TV ON THE COUCH WITH YOUR
FAMILY?

WOULD YOU RATHER...

HAVE TWO REALLY SHORT LEGS

- *OR* -

HAVE ONE LEG SHORTER THAN THE OTHER?

BE ABLE TO DRAW AMAZINGLY WELL

- *OR* -

BE ABLE TO SING REALLY, REALLY WELL?

WOULD YOU RATHER...

A GO TO COSTUME PARTY

- *OR* -

TO A TEA PARTY?

HAVE AN AUNT THAT PATS YOUR HEAD A LOT
- *OR* -
HAVE AN AUNT THAT PULLS YOUR CHEEKS
A LOT?

WOULD YOU RATHER...

BE BITTEN BY A MOSQUITO 10 TIMES

- *OR* -

BE STUNG BY A BEE 1 TIME?

THROW UP ON YOUR CRUSH

- *OR* -

THROW UP ON YOUR BEST FRIEND?

WOULD YOU RATHER...

LOOK LIKE AN OLD PERSON

- OR -

SOUND LIKE AN OLD PERSON?

SWIM IN ICE-COLD WATER

- OR -

SWIM IN A POOL OF HOT WATER?

WOULD YOU RATHER...

GET A FREE PLANE TICKET

- *OR* -

GET A FREE BOAT CRUISE?

BE ABLE RUN ON WATER

- *OR* -

BE ABLE TO BREATHE UNDERWATER?

WOULD YOU RATHER...

NEVER EAT FAST FOOD AGAIN

- OR -

EAT FAST FOOD FOR EVERY SINGLE MEAL FOR THE REST OF YOUR LIFE?

BE PRANKED WITHH A FAKE BUG

- OR -

BE PRANKED WITH A FAKE RAT?

WOULD YOU RATHER...

STOP DRINKING ANYTHING COLD ALTOGETHER

- OR -

GET A BRAIN FREEZE EVERY TIME YOU DRANK SOMETHING COLD?

SEND A PRANK TEXT

- OR -

DO A PRANK PHONE CALL?

WOULD YOU RATHER...

SHOWER WITH HOT WATER

- OR -

SHOWER WITH COLD WATER?

BE UNABLE TO CELEBRATE HALLOWEEN

- OR -

BE UNABLE TO CELEBRATE CHRISTMAS?

WOULD YOU RATHER...

FIND LOTS OF EASTER EGGS

- OR -

MEET THE EASTER BUNNY?

HAVE TO SING EVERY TIME YOU HEARD
A SONG
- OR -
HAVE TO DANCE EVERY TIME YOU HEARD A
SONG?

WOULD YOU RATHER...

BE IN A HOUSE FILLED WITH CANDY

- OR -

BE IN A HOUSE FILLED WITH MARSHMALLOWS?

GO SKYDIVING

- OR -

GO BUNGEE JUMPING?

WOULD YOU RATHER...

HAVE SUPER STRENGTH

- *OR* -

HAVE SUPER SPEED?

LIVE IN THE SKY PERMANENTLY

- *OR* -

UNDERWATER PERMANENTLY?

WOULD YOU RATHER...

NEVER HAVE CANDY, EVER AGAIN

- *OR* -

TO ONLY EAT CANDY FOR THE REST OF YOUR LIFE?

BE STUCK IN A TOILET BECAUSE THE TOILET DOOR WON'T OPEN

- *OR* -

BE STUCK IN A TOILET BECAUSE YOUR POOP WON'T FLUSH?

WOULD YOU RATHER...

GO WITH MOM TO WORK

- *OR* -

HAVE YOUR MOM STAY AT HOME ALL DAY?

BECOME THE SIZE OF A WHALE

- *OR* -

BE SHRUNK DOWN TO THE SIZE OF A BUG?

WOULD YOU RATHER...

WEAR ANY CLOTHING OF YOUR CHOICE TO SCHOOL

- *OR* -

WEAR YOUR SCHOOL UNIFORM ALL THE TIME?

TELEPORT TO THE SURFACE OF THE MOON

- *OR* -

TO THE BOTTOM OF THE OCEAN?

WOULD YOU RATHER...

EAT ONION-FLAVORED ICE CREAM

- *OR* -

EAT CHICKEN-FLAVORED COOKIES?

PLAY INSIDE

- *OR* -

PLAY OUTSIDE?

WOULD YOU RATHER...

DRESS UP AS CARTOON CHARACTERS

- *OR* -

WATCH CARTOONS?

BE ABLE TO PLAY ANY MUSICAL INSTRUMENT
THAT THERE IS
- *OR* -
BE ABLE TO SPEAK EVERY LANGUAGE
THERE IS?

WOULD YOU RATHER...

HAVE 3 ARMS

- *OR* -

ONLY 1 LEG?

BE PART OF A SET OF TWINS

- *OR* -

PART OF A SET OF TRIPLETS?

WOULD YOU RATHER...

BE ABLE TO SEW

- OR -

BE ABLE TO KNIT?

TO HAVE EYES THAT CHANGE COLOR
DEPENDING ON THE MOOD THAT YOU'RE IN
- OR -
TO HAVE HAIR THAT CHANGES COLOR BASED
ON THE TEMPERATURE?

WOULD YOU RATHER...

WEAR UNCLEAN CLOTHES FOR A WEEK

- OR -

WEAR THE SAME OUTFIT EVERY DAY FOR A WEEK?

GO TO SUMMER CAMP

- OR -

GO TO SUMMER SCHOOL?

WOULD YOU RATHER...

STROKE A FRIENDLY LION THAT'S AWAKE

- *OR* -

AN UNFRIENDLY LION WHILE IT'S ASLEEP?

SWIM OUTDOORS
- *OR* -
SWIM INDOORS?

WOULD YOU RATHER...

CLEAN UP YOUR BATHROOM

- OR -

CLEAN UP YOUR BEDROOM?

WIN A CASH PRIZE

- OR -

WIN A MYSTERY ITEM?

WOULD YOU RATHER...

BE ABLE TO SPIT OUT FIRE

- *OR* -

BE ABLE TO SPIT OUT ICE?

JUST WATCH A FOOD FIGHT
- *OR* -
BE IN A FOOD FIGHT?

WOULD YOU RATHER...

GET LOTS OF CUDDLES

- *OR* -

GET LOTS OF HUGS?

GO CAMPING

- *OR* -

GO FISHING?

WOULD YOU RATHER...

WAKE UP EARLY

- *OR* -

GO TO BED EARLY?

HAVE A DOLPHIN FOR A BEST FRIEND
- *OR* -
BECOME A DOLPHIN YOURSELF?

WOULD YOU RATHER...

HAVE A WATER BALLOON FIGHT

- OR -

A SNOWBALL FIGHT?

HAVE A CAR THAT CAN DRIVE UNDERWATER

- OR -

HAVE A FLYING CARPET?

WOULD YOU RATHER...

HAVE 3 CATS

- *OR* -

1 DOG?

DRIVE IN A CAR
- *OR* -
FLY IN A PLANE?

WOULD YOU RATHER...

BE ABLE TO RUN AS FAST AS A CHEETAH

- OR -

BE ABLE TO CLIMB WALLS LIKE A SPIDER?

HAVE FEET SO SMALL YOU HAVE TO SHOP FOR
SHOES AT THE BABY'S DEPARTMENT
- OR -
HAVE REALLY LARGE FEET?

WOULD YOU RATHER...

LICK MILK LIKE A CAT

- *OR* -

YOURSELF LIKE A CAT?

HAVE YOUR FRIEND FORGET YOUR BIRTHDAY
- *OR* -
FORGET YOUR FRIEND'S BIRTHDAY?

WOULD YOU RATHER...

NEVER BE ABLE TO LISTEN TO MUSIC AGAIN

- *OR* -

TO ONLY BE ABLE TO LISTEN TO MUSIC FROM THE 60'S?

HAVE YELLOW EYES

- *OR* -

HAVE GREEN EYES?

WOULD YOU RATHER...

GO TO CLASS IN YOUR UNDERWEAR

- OR -

WEAR PAJAMAS TO CLASS?

NEVER HAVE TO HAVE A SHOWER EVER AGAIN
- OR -
NEVER HAVE TO BRUSH YOUR TEETH EVER
AGAIN?

WOULD YOU RATHER...

STICK WITH YOUR OLD FRIENDS AT A PARTY

- *OR* -

MAKE NEW FRIENDS AT A PARTY?

GET PRESENTS YOU DON'T LIKE ON YOUR
BIRTHDAY
- *OR* -
GET NO PRESENTS AT ALL?

WOULD YOU RATHER...

READ A HARDCOVER BOOK

- OR -

LISTEN TO AN AUDIOBOOK?

HAVE REALLY GREEN SKIN

- OR -

HAVE BLUE SKIN LIKE AN ALIEN?

WOULD YOU RATHER...

BE THE WORLD'S RICHEST PERSON

- OR -

HAVE THREE FREE WISHES?

SHARE YOUR BED WITH SOMEONE WHO TALKS
IN THEIR SLEEP
- OR -
SHARE YOUR BED WITH SOMEONE WHO
SNORES?

WOULD YOU RATHER...

GO TO A CLOTHING STORE

- OR -

TO A TOY STORE?

HAVE NO EYEBROWS
- OR -
HAVE PINK EYEBROWS?

WOULD YOU RATHER...

HAVE A NEWLY DISCOVERED ANIMAL NAMED AFTER YOU

- OR -

HAVE A NEW CANDY NAMED AFTER YOU?

BE TOO OCOLD AT NIGHT

- OR -

BE TOO HOT AT NIGHT?

WOULD YOU RATHER...

SNEAK INTO YOUR NEIGHBOR'S HOUSE WHILE
THEY'RE ASLEEP

- *OR* -

SPY ON YOUR NEIGHBOR?

SCRATCH YOUR BUTT IN PUBLIC
- *OR* -
SCRATCH YOUR ARMPIT IN PUBLIC?

WOULD YOU RATHER...

MEET AN ALIEN

- OR -

MEET GOD?

HAVE POOP THAT SMELLS LIKE STRAWBERRY

- OR -

BE ABLE TO POOP CHOCOLATE?

WOULD YOU RATHER...

HAVE A LIBRARY IN YOUR HOUSE

- *OR* -

GO TO THE LIBRARY?

BUILD A HAPPY SNOWMAN

- *OR* -

BUILD AN AWESOME SAND CASTLE?

WOULD YOU RATHER...

HAVE AN ITCH THAT REFUSES TO GO AWAY

- OR -

HAVE AN ITCH YOU CAN'T SCRATCH?

JUST ONE SUPERPOWER FOR A MONTH

- OR -

HAVE A LOT OF SUPERPOWERS FOR ONE WEEK?

WOULD YOU RATHER...

HAVE THE ABILITY TO BECOME INVISIBLE

- *OR* -

HAVE THE POWER TO READ PEOPLE'S MINDS?

FALL ASLEEP IN CLASS

- *OR* -

FALL ASLEEP ON THE BUS?

WOULD YOU RATHER...

GO JOGGING

- *OR* -

GO RUNNING?

GET INTO TROUBLE WITH YOUR PARENTS OVER
SOMETHING YOU DIDN'T DO
- *OR* -
SNITCH ON YOUR BEST FRIEND ABOUT
SOMETHING THEY DID?

WOULD YOU RATHER...

HAVE TISSUE PAPER STUCK TO THE BOTTOM OF YOUR SHOE

- *OR* -

HAVE GUM STUCK TO THE BOTTOM OF YOUR SHOE?

BE POPULAR AMONG YOUR CLASSMATES

- *OR* -

BE POPULAR AMONG YOUR TEACHERS?

WOULD YOU RATHER...

RELAX BESIDE THE POOL

- *OR* -

GO SWIMMING?

FART IN AN ELEVATOR ON YOUR WAY TO
CLASS
- *OR* -
FART IN CLASS?

WOULD YOU RATHER...

BE STUCK IN A BOAT IN THE MIDDLE OF THE OCEAN

- *OR* -

BE STUCK ON A ROCKETSHIP FLOATING THROUGH SPACE?

HAVE A GIANT POOL
- *OR* -
HAVE A JACUZZI?

WOULD YOU RATHER...

BE GIVEN $10 EVERY SINGLE DAY FOR THE REST OF YOUR LIFE

- OR -

GIVEN $1,000 ONLY ONCE?

OWN 10 PUPPIES
- OR -
10 KITTENS?

WOULD YOU RATHER...

BE SURPRISED WITH A PONY

- *OR* -

FIND A PONY ON YOUR OWN?

EAT SOMETHING ROASTED

- *OR* -

EAT SOMETHING FRIED?

WOULD YOU RATHER...

CREEP INTO YOUR SIBLING'S ROOM AND SNUGGLE UP WITH THEM

- *OR* -

SLEEP ALONE WHEN IT'S RAINING HEAVILY?

HAVE A TUMMY THAT MAKES RUMBLING NOISES A LOT

- *OR* -

HAVE A REALLY FAT TUMMY?

WOULD YOU RATHER...

HAVE A REALLY LOUD VOICE

- *OR* -

HAVE A SQUEAKY VOICE?

HAVE ALL THE JUNK FOOD YOU COULD
EVER WANT
- *OR* -
HAVE ALL THE DRINKS YOU COULD EVER
WANT?

WOULD YOU RATHER...

LICK YOUR FOOT

- *OR* -

YOUR FRIEND'S FOOT?

MOVE TO A NEW HOUSE
- *OR* -
GO TO A NEW SCHOOL?

WOULD YOU RATHER...

NOT GET ANY FOOD TO EAT FOR AN ENTIRE WEEKEND

- OR -

EAT FOOD OUT OF THE TRASHCAN?

WORK AS A LION TAMER

- OR -

NOT WORK AT ALL AND HAVE A PET MONKEY?

WOULD YOU RATHER...

MEET A FRIENDLY DINOSAUR

- *OR* -

MEET A FRIENDLY DRAGON?

HAVE BRIGHT GREEN HAIR
- *OR* -
BRIGHT PINK HAIR?

WOULD YOU RATHER...

BE THE RULER OF ANY OTHER COUNTRY IN THE WORLD

- OR -

BE THE PRESIDENT OF THE UNITED STATES?

NOT BE ABLE TO TASTE ANYTHING

- OR -

NOT BE ABLE TO SMELL ANYTHING?

WOULD YOU RATHER...

BRUSH YOUR TEETH WITH KETCHUP

- *OR* -

WITH HOT SAUCE?

HAVE A SNAIL AS A PET
- *OR* -
EAT A SNAIL?

WOULD YOU RATHER...

HAVE LARGE HANDS

- *OR* -

HAVE LARGE FEET?

STAY YOUNG FOREVER
- *OR* -
GROW UP INTO AN ADULT OVERNIGHT?

WOULD YOU RATHER...

EAT ON THE LIVING ROOM COUCH

- *OR* -

EAT IN YOUR BED?

LIVE IN A REALLY NOISY NEIGHBORHOOD
- *OR* -
IN A REALLY QUIET NEIGHBORHOOD?

WOULD YOU RATHER...

GO FISHING

- OR -

GO HIKING?

KNOW HOW TO SPEAK SPANISH FLUENTLY
- OR -
KNOW HOW TO SPEAK FRENCH FLUENTLY?

WOULD YOU RATHER...

NEVER BE ABLE TO SMELL AGAIN

- OR -

BE ABLE TO SMELL ONLY BAD-SMELLING THINGS?

FORGET YOU HAVE FEARS
- OR -
FACE YOUR FEARS?

WOULD YOU RATHER...

KNOW HOW TO READ LIPS

- OR -

KNOW AND UNDERSTAND SIGN LANGUAGE?

HAVE HAIR THAT'S ALMOST TOUCHING THE
FLOOR
- OR -
BE BALD?

WOULD YOU RATHER...

LIVE IN A BOAT ON THE OPEN OCEAN

- OR -

IN A TREE HOUSE FOR THE REST OF YOUR LIFE?

EAT YOUR FINGERNAILS

- OR -

YOUR TOENAILS?

WOULD YOU RATHER...

NEVER HAVE PIZZA, EVER AGAIN

- *OR* -

EAT A YEAR'S WORTH OF PIZZA IN A SINGE NIGHT?

BE ON A TINY BOAT
- *OR* -
ON A GIANT SHIP?

WOULD YOU RATHER...

GO SEE A REAL LIFE SHIP

- *OR* -

GET A TOY BOAT?

HAVE A PET DINOSAUR

- *OR* -

HAVE A PET DRAGON?

WOULD YOU RATHER...

BE SURROUNDED BY ANNOYING PEOPLE

- OR -

HAVE NO FRIENDS?

TO READ REALLY SLOWLY, BUT UNDERSTAND
WHAT YOU READ REALLY FAST
- OR -
BE ABLE TO READ REALLY FAST, BUT NOT
UNDERSTAND IT?

WOULD YOU RATHER...

LOOK REALLY OLD

- *OR* -

LIKE A NEWBORN BABY AGAIN?

BE IN A DISNEY MOVIE

- *OR* -

BE IN A DISNEY ANIMATION?

WOULD YOU RATHER...

FLY IN THE SKY WITH THE BIRDS

- *OR* -

SWIM IN THE OPEN OCEAN WITH THE DOLPHINS?

PET A GIRAFFE
- *OR* -
PET A HIPPOPOTAMUS?

Printed in the USA
CPSIA information can be obtained
at www.ICGtesting.com
LVHW090722191123
764340LV00033B/464